Set Two
Workbook Two

By David Orme

Accompanies the Boffin Boy reading books

- Boffin Boy and the Rock Men
- Boffin Boy and the Quest for Wisdom
- Boffin Boy and the Temples of Mars.

Ransom

Boffin Boy Set Two Workbook Two
by David Orme

Illustrated by Peter Richardson

Published by Ransom Publishing Ltd.
51 Southgate Street, Winchester Hants. SO23 9EH UK
www.ransom.co.uk

ISBN 978 184167 708 8
First published in 2008

A CIP catalogue record of this book is available from the British Library.

Design and layout: www.macwiz.co.uk

Find out more about Boffin Boy at www.ransom.co.uk

Contents

Introduction

The purpose of this material is to provide opportunities to check pupils' understanding of the Boffin Boy stories and to provide structures to encourage writing in a range of forms.

Pupils working at the reading level assumed by these books frequently have a mis-match between their experiential oral skills and their skills in reading and writing. The Boffin Boy stories and support materials are intended to be:

- appealing and engaging, particularly to those who may be otherwise reluctant to read, but appropriate as a fun read for all pupils;
- highly visual, with minimum text in the stories and minimum rubric on the worksheets;
- age appropriate;
- achievable; and
- appropriately challenging.

This Workbook covers three of the Boffin Boy titles: *Boffin Boy and the Rock Men, Boffin Boy and the Quest for Wisdom and Boffin Boy and the Temples of Mars*. There are eight worksheets for each title, plus five sheets of artwork resources that pupils can use in various ways, including designing their own Boffin Boy graphic novels. Further ideas for these are provided in the teacher's notes. The worksheets have a literacy focus, but include a range of lighter, fun activities such as word searches and code-breaking. The sheets are introduced by a character from the story and, in keeping with the stories, are slightly more wacky and offbeat than the traditional literacy worksheet!

Each sheet is fully supported by teacher's notes. For these pupils it is essential that the work on the sheets is prepared as a class or group exercise, and suggestions for this are provided (suggestions include oral work and shared writing). Simply handing out the sheets, perhaps as a homework exercise, is unlikely to be successful.

Worksheet 1 – Instruction Sheet

Task:

Write a set of instructions for using your Rock Man.

Support:

Find examples of instructions (e.g. video recorder, mobile phone, MP3 player) and discuss the style used – i.e. the use of the imperative, chronological ordering, etc.

Discuss each section on the Worksheet. What will be in the first section? (Inserting batteries, talking to your Rock Man for the first time.)

Pupils will need to come up with their own ideas for some of the headings (e.g. 'What you can do with your Rock Man'), as this information is not included in the text – perhaps because the Rock Men don't do very much anyway!

Extension:

Write a set of instructions for the product devised in Worksheet 6 (Get Rich!). Produce it as a leaflet.

Worksheet 2 – Love It or Hate It

Task:

Stating an opinion; writing persuasive text.

Support:

Discuss why Colonel Bullet has fallen for his Rock Man, and why Wu Pee hates his. The writing should have logical progression, rather than just being a list of ideas – pupils could draft their ideas first.

In the second part of the task, the two characters offer reasons why they think other people should (or should not) have a Rock Man. Again, pupils should draft some cogent points before starting the writing.

Extension:

Use the same format to write about other items – e.g. mobile phone, MP3 player. In particular, ask pupils to come up with strong arguments against the particular item, even if they are very much in favour of it.

More able pupils might like to write their opinion on why many people think it is important to own the latest gadgets, designer-label clothes, etc.

Worksheet 3 – Hand Over Your Rock Men!

Task:

Writing a play script.

Support:

Improvise the conversation before starting the writing. This activity should allow pupils to marshal the arguments on both sides. As suggested in the text of the Worksheet, additional characters can be included – e.g. Boffin Boy, the child's dad.

Ensure that pupils are familiar with the conventions of play scripts.

Extension:

The child's parents have destroyed the Rock Man, but Boffin Boy's upgrade makes them safe. Write the second part of the play, in which the same child demands a new Rock Man.

Worksheet 4 – Planet News – News Story

Task:

Write the newspaper story 'Destroy all Rock Men.'

Support:

Ensure that pupils are familiar with the conventions of newspaper journalism – e.g. the use of indirect speech and the use of sub headlines.

Remind pupils of the point in the story at which the newspaper appears: this is after Rock Men have been found to be dangerous, but before it is discovered who is responsible. This 'angle' should be brought out in the newspaper story, perhaps with sub heads – e.g. 'Who is responsible?' or 'Boffin Boy on the case'.

Extension:

Write a further newspaper report appropriate for the end of the story, when all the facts have been revealed.

Worksheet 5 – Red Wolf's Scam

Task:

Retelling the story from the point of view of Red Wolf.

Support:

The retelling is supported with just an opening sentence and a Word box. Further support can be given by asking appropriate questions – e.g. How well did the plan work? How did Red Wolf plan to get the money? What gave him away? How was he defeated?

Extension:

Write an additional paragraph in which Red Wolf plans his escape, perhaps with the unwitting help of the not-so-bright computer DAVE.

Worksheet 6 – Get Rich!

Task:

Devise a 'get rich quick' scheme by inventing the next Christmas craze.

Support:

This would work best as a pair/group planning and discussion activity. Each group could then present their ideas. Some starter ideas are included on the Worksheet.

Extension:

A discussion/debate on the strategies that different manufacturers use to manipulate consumers into buying designer labels, new gadgets, etc. This can then lead on to the next activity.

Worksheet 7 – Rock Men Advert

Task:

Devise a TV advertisement for the Rock Men.

Support:

Discuss the various elements that can be used to make up a TV advert. These include using 'voice-over' scripts, slogan texts, 'mini-dramas' involving characters – sometimes celebrities, exciting visuals, and the use of humour and powerful slogans to make the product memorable.

Which of these elements would be particularly effective in promoting the Rock Men (i.e. in encouraging peer pressure and pester power in advertisements aimed at children)?

Ask pupils to work in groups to develop their ideas.

Extension:

Develop ideas for a TV advertisement for the 'Get Rich Quick!' product worked on in Worksheet Six.

Worksheet 8 – Write a Picture Brief

Task:

Write a picture brief.

Support:

Discuss what information will be needed for the picture, including a general overview sentence. Will the author need to supply a description for Colonel Bullet? (No – the artist has already drawn him. But this is the first time we have met Colonel Bullet's mum in the books.)

Stress the importance of describing facial expressions and posture for the two characters.

For the second activity, pupils may find it helpful to draw the invention first.

Extension:

Ask pupils to write a picture brief for other pupils to work up as a drawing.

1 Getting started

2 Things you can do with your Rock Man

3 Looking after your Rock Man

4 How to connect your Rock Man to your computer

5 What happens to your Rock Man when you are online

Worksheet 2: Love It or Hate It

Colonel Bullet loved his Rock Man – but Wu Pee didn't! Why do you think that was?

I loved my Rock Man because

I think everyone should have one because

I hated the thing because

Don't waste your money, because

It wasn't easy making kids give up their Rock Men! Can you finish this play script? Check out the story to see what they say, and use these words in your script. You could add in more characters if you wish – for example, maybe the boy in the picture rings me up to check out the newspaper report. Oh, and you had better think up a name for him.

Mum	**Hand over that Rock Man!**
....	**No chance!**
Mum	
....	

Can you write this news story? You can include more pictures if you like – you know Boffin Boy always likes to be in the newspapers! Or maybe you could have a picture of Red Wolf.

PLANET NEWS

DESTROY ALL ROCK MEN!

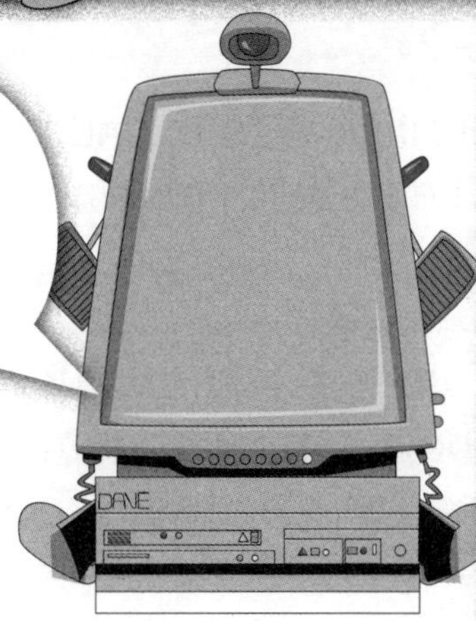

Boffin Boy left that Red Wolf with me, in Boffin Boy's secret laboratory. Red Wolf told me all about his Rock Men scam. He's a smart guy, that Red Wolf!

Word box
- hypnotise
- LUBRA
- Christmas
- craze
- Internet
- credit card
- success
- Boffin Boy
- Wu Pee
- vat
- covered
- trapped

"I had this brilliant idea to get loads of cash! First, I took over a factory in Zone City. Getting people to work there would cost me money, so I …

Worksheet 6: Get Rich!

I am a brilliant Ninja wizard, and I know many secrets. Here is the secret of making a load of cash!

Come up with the next big Christmas craze!
It could be a computer game, a toy, a new type of mobile phone, an electronic gadget, or something else …

What your idea is called ______________________

What it looks like

What it does

Why it will be really popular

Rock Men Ad – Planning Sheet

A good slogan for the Rock Men

....

What sort of music the advert should have

....

What the advert should show

....

....

....

....

Voice-over script

....

....

....

....

....

....

....

....

When the books were written, the author, David Orme, had to explain to the illustrator, Peter Richardson, what was to be in each of the pictures. This explanation is called a picture brief. David didn't explain every detail of each picture. He wanted Peter to come up with his own ideas, as well.

Write a picture brief for this illustration:

In this picture, Colonel Bullet ....

....

....

....

....

....

....

Here's another brief:

Boffin Boy invents something new!

What is it?

What does it do?

Write a picture brief for it.

Worksheet 1 – How Wu Pee Searched for Wisdom

Task:

To outline the events of the story from the point of view of Wu Pee.

Support:

The worksheet provides structured support for a retelling of the story. Provide a word list if needed.

For a more challenging task, replace the sentences with fewer words – e.g. First … , I found … , So I … , but … , I tried … , then … , luckily … , in the end … .

Extension:

Use the same approach for a retelling of the story from the point of view of Boffin Boy. This time, pupils will have to come up with their own starter words.

Worksheet 2 – Book Review

Task:

Write a book review of Boffin Boy and the Quest for Wisdom.

Support:

A framework for the review is provided on the sheet, but the activity would benefit from an initial discussion. Ensure that pupils know that the 'blurb' is the descriptive text that appears on the back cover of the book.

Extension:

The notes made on the sheet could form the basis of a more formally written book review.

This worksheet can be adapted for use with other titles in the series.

Worksheet 3 – Kidnapping Wu Pee

Task:

Explanation text – devising a range of plans for the kidnapping of Wu Pee.

Support:

Pupils need to come up with two original ideas for the first two speech bubbles. The third speech bubble should contain the plan as it is described in the book, but it should be written in the same form as the other two ideas.

The two original ideas can be as bizarre and as imaginative as is wished.

For more able pupils, the sheet could be used for notes, to be expanded on a separate sheet.

Extension:

Work out a more detailed plan, perhaps with timings, a list of resources required, etc.

Worksheet 4 – Pitching a Programme

Task:

To write persuasive text on an idea for a new TV show.

Support:

Explain that before a TV show is made, the company producing it has to persuade a broadcaster that it is a good idea. This is called a 'pitch.' The key part of the pitch is to persuade the broadcaster that lots of people will want to watch it.

Extension:

Encourage pupils to come up with their own ideas for a reality show, then use the format on the sheet to say why it is a good idea.

Worksheet 5 – A Wizard Timetable

Task:

To produce a list of subjects to be studied at Bog Street School for Wizards, and to explain why they are studied.

Support:

Some subjects are already suggested on the worksheet, but the notes for these are incomplete. There is also further space for pupils' own ideas for subjects to study.

Pupils will probably quickly realise that this part of the story is a sly reference to other stories involving schools for wizards. This may provide some ideas. The task can be taken more or less seriously. (Since Bog Street School for Wizards lacks the glamour of other, better-known schools for wizards, the subjects studied may be equally less glamorous!)

Extension:

Pupils could draw up a weekly timetable for the school, using ICT to make it look appropriately wizard-like.

Worksheet 6 – Cracking the Code

Task:

Cracking the code of reversed and mirrored letters.

Support:

This is a straight-forward activity. In the first two codes the messages are written in reverse. The third code is in mirror writing, with the letters themselves reversed.

Extension:

Pupils may like to try writing their own messages in reverse or mirror writing.

Worksheet 7 – Illustrator's Brief

Task:

Writing a description of a picture.

Support:

Explain that this picture will need to be described in detail, as the illustrator will be familiar with only one of the characters – Wu Pee – who does not need to be described. The support on the sheet encourages an overview statement before writing about the detail of the sheet.

Extension:

Writing briefs for other pages. Writing a brief for an imaginary Boffin Boy scene, for other pupils to draw.

Worksheet 8 – Dave Gets it Wrong

Task:

Sequencing the events of the story and a cloze activity.

Support:

Pupils could start by numbering each of the eight statements, then writing them on the lines below before filling in the missing words.

Extension:

Dave malfunctions even more. Ask pupils to write sentences about the story, then muddle the words and ask other pupils to rearrange them to find the original sentences.

First of all, I used a disguise to …

I found …

So I …

The trouble was, I couldn't …

I tried …

Then these celebrities heard about it, and they …

Boffin Boy got me out of it by …

Even DAVE couldn't crack the code. Can you?

The code says……………………………………………………………………………

Worksheet 2: Book Review

My favourite part was when

because

The funniest part of the story was

I would have liked to have read more about the scene when

The story would have been better if

My blurb for Boffin Boy and the Search for Wisdom would be

People kept saying that we were really dumb, so we decided to steal the secret of wisdom from Wu Pee! First of all, we had to come up with a plan! My plan was the one we went for.

My idea is to

I think that we ought to

I've got a better idea! First, we need to wait until Wu Pee

If a company that makes TV programmes has an idea for a new show, they have to convince people that it's a good idea. There's no point in making a show if no-one wants to watch it!

Bling TV want to make a programme called Celebrity Crocodile Wrestling.

BLING TV

Use this sheet for your ideas about the show, then write your 'pitch' to sell the show.

Name of show: Celebrity Crocodile Wrestling

What will happen on the show:

What sort of celebrities might take part:

Why it's a really good idea for a show:

That Wu Pee came to teach us at Bog Street School for Wizards. He was a right weirdo, if you ask me.
What do you think we study at our school for wizards?

Bog Street School for Wizards: List of Subjects

Shapeshifting

Teaching you how to turn yourself into an animal, or … well, anything you like really.
Useful when

Making deadly poisons

Really good for

But be careful that

Becoming invisible

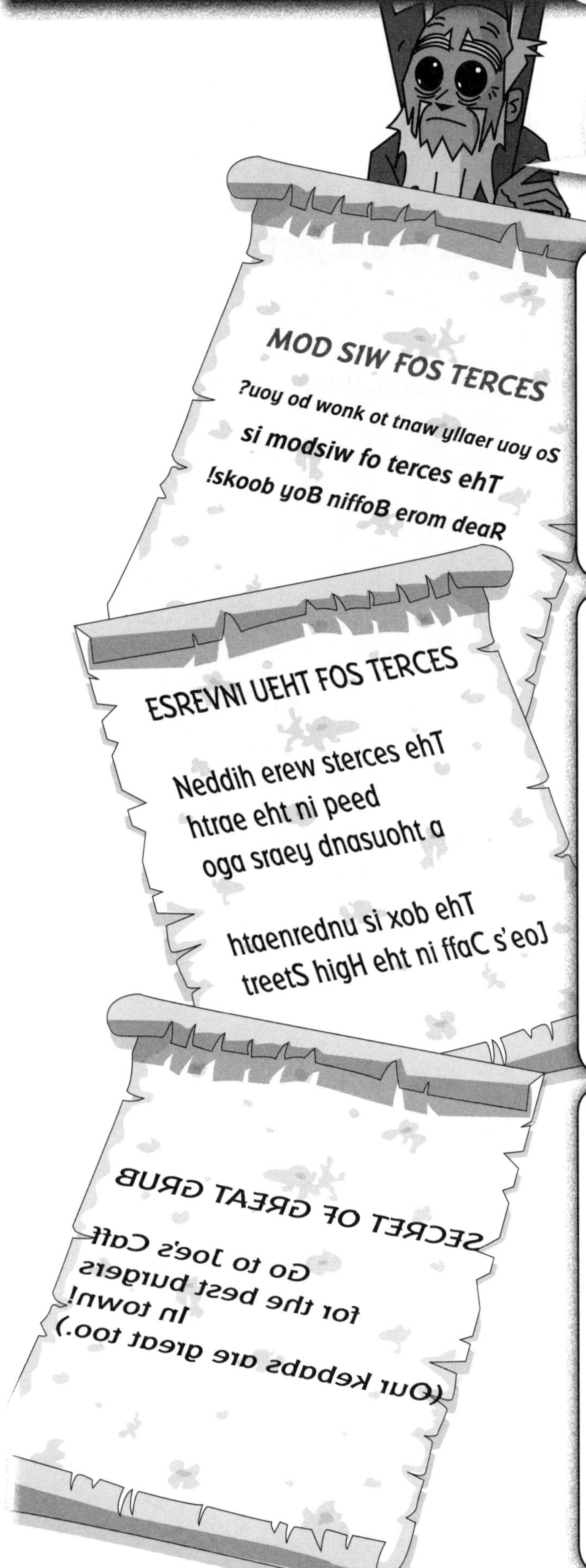

I still can't crack this code – and what's worse, I've just found some more secret parchments! Can you help?

This message says

This message says

This message says

This scene is set in a ....

shop. Behind the counter is ....

Dave the computer has got this story in a muddle! Can you write it in the correct order, and fill in the missing words?

Boffin Boy had a new computer called D………. .

Wu Pee was looking for ancient w……………… .

Wu Pee was rescued by B……………… B……. .

He found an old p……………………… in a library.

Even D………. couldn't crack the c……… .

They k………………………Wu Pee.

He couldn't crack the c…………. .

A secret society of c…………………… wanted the secret.

The correct version is

Worksheet 1 – The Thoughts of Wu Pee

Task:

To complete thought bubbles for various points in the story.

Support:

Begin by discussing Wu Pee's thoughts and anxieties at the various points in the story – e.g. on the journey to Mars (he's bored and really doesn't want to be going there); when Boffin Boy opens the air lock door (he's worried that something awful might be on the other side), etc.

Extension:

Find other points in the story where thought bubbles from any of the characters might usefully comment on the story. These pages could then be created using the photocopiable picture resource pages.

Worksheet 2 – The Wise Ones Tell the Story

Task:

To retell the narrative from the point of view of the Wise Ones.

Support:

This is a straightforward activity, with scaffolding provided on the sheet. For a more challenging task, blank out all of the sentence starters except the first two.

Extension:

Carry out a similar task for the crisis described in Worksheet 5.

Worksheet 3 – Space Ship Review

Task:

Write a review of the two space ships in the story.

Support:

Pupils will need to be familiar with the language, format and content of new car reviews.
If possible, provide examples of this from magazines. Encourage pupils not to take the task too seriously – the reviews can be along the lines of the Wise Ones' comments in the story.

Extension:

Write a review of the Wise Ones' comet-smashing device, or an invention from one of the other Boffin Boy stories.

Worksheet 4 – Facts about Mars

Task:

This activity asks pupils to write a brief encyclopaedia entry for Mars, using the muddled notes on the sheet as a starting point.

Support:

Work through the disjointed facts, linking related facts (e.g. the moon information) and thinking about an appropriate order – e.g. size and position in the Solar System, the moons, conditions on the surface, possibility of life. Pupils should then be able to write the entry.

Extension:

Pupils could produce an extended encyclopaedia entry by researching further information on the Internet – e.g. by visiting websites such as www.nasa.gov.

Worksheet 5 – Another Crisis

Task:

To describe a second crisis requiring the intervention of the Wise Ones.

Support:

Various crises, sensible and ridiculous, are suggested, but there is space available for pupils to come up with their own ideas. A good approach would be for pupils to write about the crisis as a series of bullet points.

Encourage pupils to be as humorous and/or imaginative as possible in their solutions to the crisis.

Extension:

The new crisis can be written up as a story, either in text form or as a graphic novel.

Worksheet 6 – News Headlines

Task:

To write newspaper headlines as they might appear on Earth from the point when the comet in the story is sighted.

Support:

Look at a range of headlines from different newspapers. How different would a tabloid and a serious newspaper headline be in this case? How are headlines worded to provide the most impact? Pupils could provide two sets of headlines, one representing a tabloid and one a serious newspaper.

Use the discussion to provide a word list to support the activity. Some of the words could be drawn from the headlines studied.

Extension:

Write the news reports that go with the headlines.

Worksheet 7 – A Different Ending

Task:

Creative writing - making notes for a different ending to the story.

Support:

The new ending starts at the point when Boffin Boy opens the door to discover the sleeping Wise Ones.

Begin by discussing possibilities for the different story ending, perhaps making lists of good and bad things that could be behind the door.

Remind pupils that the object is to produce a story, so a poisonous gas or murdering beast that wipes out our heroes is not a sensible choice. Suggest, for example, that Boffin Boy and Wu Pee are captured, and the story is based around their escape.

Extension:

Expand the notes made into a story, either using continuous text or a graphic novel approach.

Worksheet 8 – Crossword

Task:

To complete the crossword on a Martian theme.

Support:

The task is a straightforward one, though weaker pupils may require further help beyond the clues provided.

A good approach is to ask pupils to work in pairs.

Extension:

Select other words from the text (or relating to Mars) and ask pupils to come up with crossword-style definitions for other pupils to solve.

Solution:

Across: 1 Solar 2 Beam 6 Temple 8 Mars 9 Aid 11 Building 12 Danger

Down: 1 System 3 Earth 4 Magic 5 Spell 7 Martian 9 Ago 10 Dust

Worksheet 1: The Thoughts of Wu Pee

What do you think I'm thinking at each of these points in the story?

1. On the way to Mars …

2. When Boffin Boy wanted to open the air lock in the Temple …

3. At this very serious moment in the story …

4. At the very end of the story …

When we got back to Mars, we wrote down in the Great Book of the Ancient Ones what had happened when we met Boffin Boy and Wu Pee! This is what we wrote (well, some of it!).

We were woken by travellers from Earth. Here is a description of them.

They told us that the Earth …

Their space ship was …

So we …

We took off into space, and were able to …

…………………… seemed pretty smart, so we gave him ……………………

WHAT SPACE SHIP is my all-time favourite mag!

WHAT SPACE SHIP Issue 132

Top spaceman Dan Mekon reviews two space ships.

The BOFF 1

This space ship was designed by the Snurgons. It

STAR RATING ☆

The Wise Ones' space ship

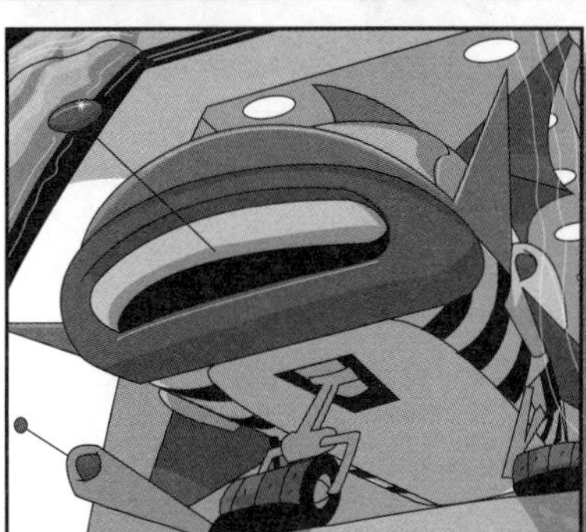

This ship was designed by the Wise Men of Mars. It

STAR RATING ☆ ☆ ☆ ☆ ☆

These facts about Mars are all in a muddle!
Can you use them to write an entry for my brilliant ON-LINE encyclopaedia WuPeedia?

Fourth planet from the sun	Very cold	Phobos and Deimos	Smaller than the Earth	Once had water on the surface
Dust storms	Two moons	May have been life once	Thin atmosphere	Some simple life may still be there

http://www.wupeedia.com/mars

Mars

Welcome to WUPEEDIA the free encyclopaedia.

There is another crisis on Earth! We are going to have to wake the Wise Ones up again!

What could the crisis be?

- Earth invaded by really nasty aliens.
- Climate change gets worse.
- A super volcano erupts.
- Wu Pee runs out of tea bags again.
- ....
- ....
- ....

What the Wise Ones did to solve the crisis:

....

....

....

....

....

....

....

....

Scientists on Earth spotted the comet heading for them – and there were really big newspaper headlines about it!

Can you write these headlines for Planet News?

PLANET NEWS

Headline One – When scientists first spot the comet, and don't know whether it will hit the Earth.

PLANET NEWS

Headline Two – When they know that the comet will destroy the Earth in three days time.

PLANET NEWS

Headline Three – News of how people behaved on Earth.

PLANET NEWS

Headline Four – When the comet was blown to bits.

PLANET NEWS

Headline Five – When they found out that it was Boffin Boy that had saved the World.

This is the point in the story where I get to open the air lock door. I had no idea what we might find inside! Use this page to plan out your own story about what happened when we opened the door …

What happened when the door was opened?

When they went inside, what did they see?

What did Wu Pee say?

What did Boffin Boy say?

What happened next?

What happened in the end?

The answers to this crossword are all connected with the story.

Crossword clues

Across

1. The sun and planets make up this. (and 1 down)
2. A word for a ray of light – or a big piece of wood!
6. A holy building – Boffin Boy found one on Mars.
8. The fourth planet from the Sun.
9. The Wise Men come to _ _ _ the Earth.
11. There are many different sorts, but it always has walls and a roof! Boffin Boy found one on Mars.
12. What a red light means – this never worries Boffin Boy.

Down

1. The sun and planets make up this. (and 1 across)
3. The third planet from the Sun – useful to grow plants in.
4. Wu Pee can sometimes do this.
5. Wu Pee's books are full of these. Also what you do to get words right.
7. One of these might live on 8 across.
9. The Wise Ones reached Mars a long time …
10. There is lots of this stuff on the surface of Mars.

The following five picture resource pages are provided to enable pupils to undertake a variety of tasks in a more creative way.

The following are merely some starting point suggestions for their use:

1. Cut out appropriate pictures of the villains. Create 'Wanted Posters'.
2. Design appropriate backgrounds for one of the stories from the books, or for a new story. Then cut out appropriate characters to illustrate a scene from the book or story.
3. Use the characters, objects and speech / thought bubbles to mock up a page using the graphic novel style.
4. Discuss possible alternative endings for stories, and continue the story in graphic novel format.
5. Develop a board game based on one of the books. Use the characters to produce cards. Create further cards to illustrate weapons.
6. Create puzzles in the same styles as those in the workbooks – word searches, codes, etc.
7. Devise maps for various locations described in the books. Illustrate with appropriate characters.
8. Use as illustrations for pupils' own stories.
9. Design Web pages, perhaps by scanning the images and using them in an appropriate design program.

Graphic Novels and ICT

Microsoft Word provides facilities for pupils to design their own graphic novel pages. Objects such as clip art or pupils' own scanned pictures can be imported into the page.

A range of callouts (speech and thought bubbles) are included in Microsoft Word, and can be pasted in. To find them, open the Drawing toolbar, click on Autoshapes then Callouts. Text can then be placed in the callouts, which can be dragged into position.

In addition, the Drawing toolbar offers a Word Art feature ideal for 'sound effect' words such as 'Kaboom!' Text boxes can be used for caption boxes in the pages, and both text boxes and the callouts can have colour fills.

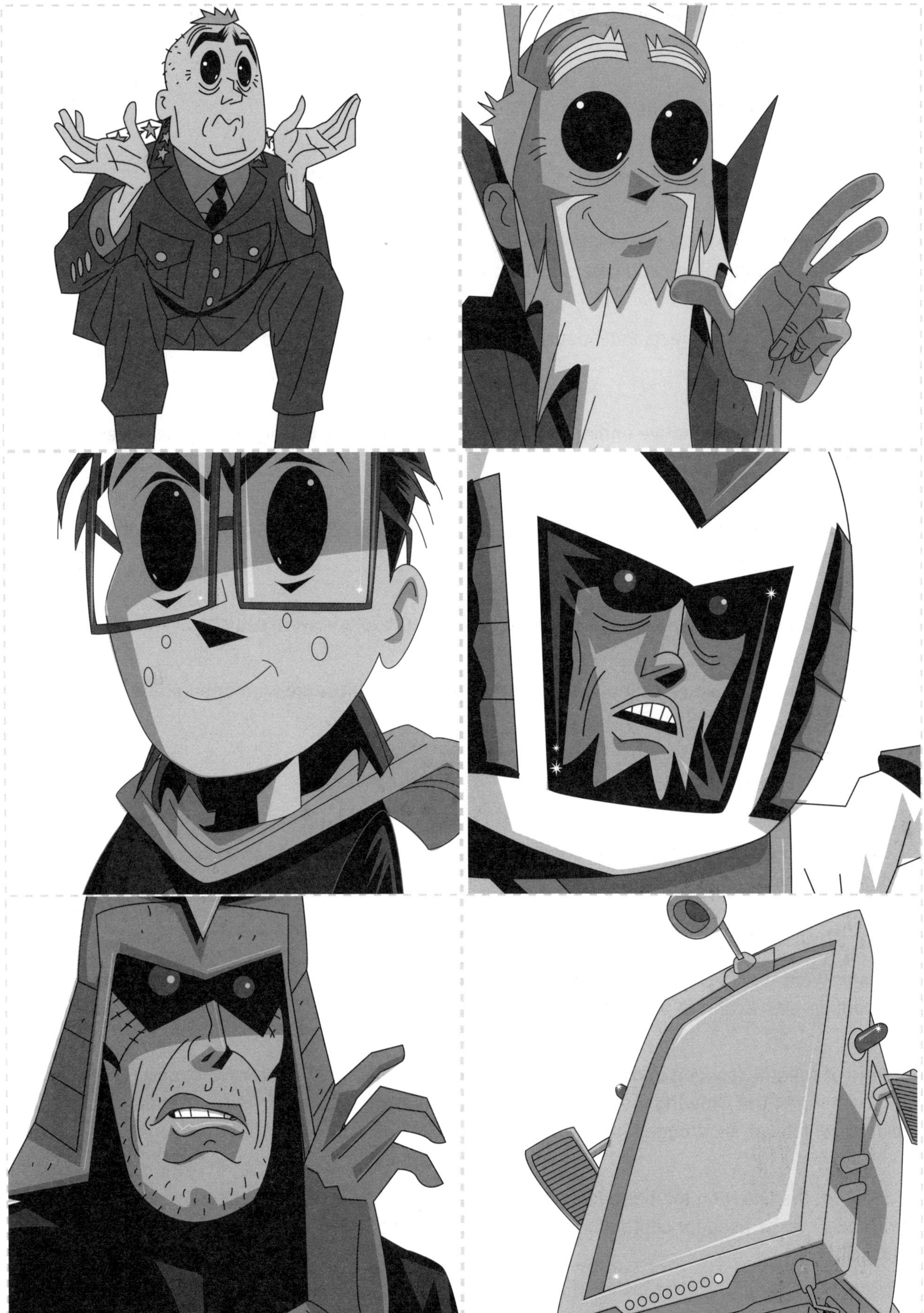

ROCKMEN
ROCKMEN
ROCKMEN

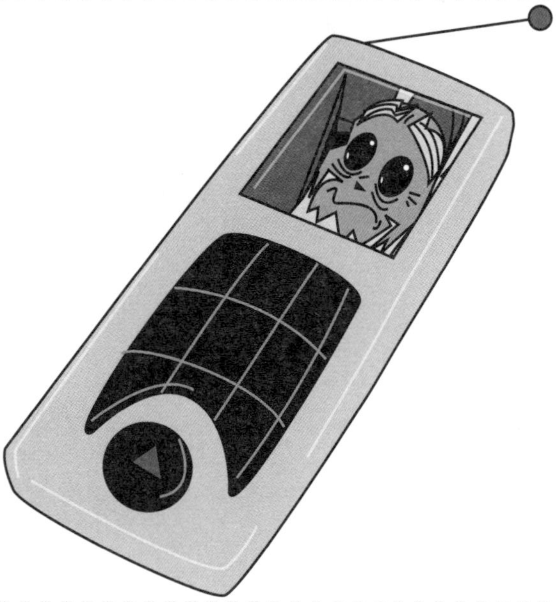

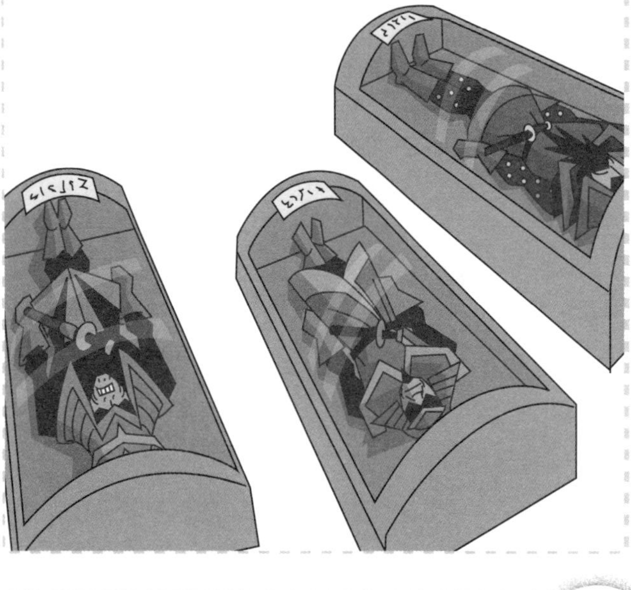

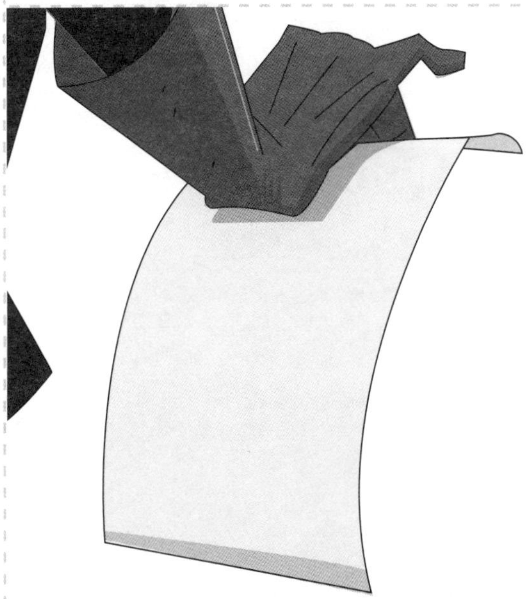